Maths
made easy

Key Stage 2
ages 7-8
Advanced

D0620378

Author and Consultant Sean McArdle

Certificate ☆ ☆ ☆ ★

Congratulations to ....

(write your name here)

for successfully finishing this book.

☆ *You're a star!* ☆

DK

LONDON • NEW YORK • MUNICH • MELBOURNE • DELHI

Ordering

Write these numbers in order starting with the smallest.

| 670 | 760 | 607 | 706 |

| *607* | *670* | *706* | *760* |

Write these numbers in order starting with the smallest.

270	720	207	702

870	780	807	708

906	690	960	609

106	610	601	160

560	506	650	605

849	489	948	984

890	980	809	908

486	684	864	648

405	450	540	504

746	647	764	674

570	586	490	92

76	104	200	92

440	66	781	177

632	236	77	407

842	587	99	88

74	101	12	800

500	468	395	288

600	304	403	89

78	9	302	470

345	543	53	34

Tenths

Write the fractions for the shaded squares on the bar.

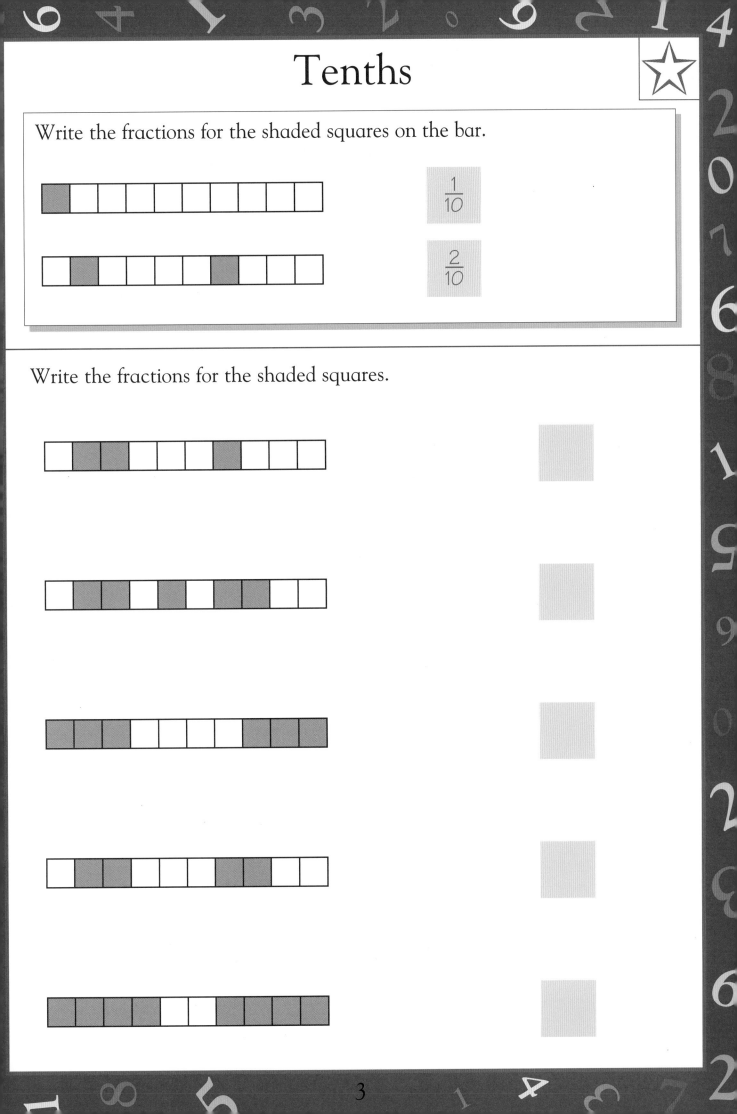

$\frac{1}{10}$

$\frac{2}{10}$

Write the fractions for the shaded squares.

3

Comparing fractions

Compare the shaded fractions of these blocks. Write < (sign for is less than) or > (sign for is more than) in the box.

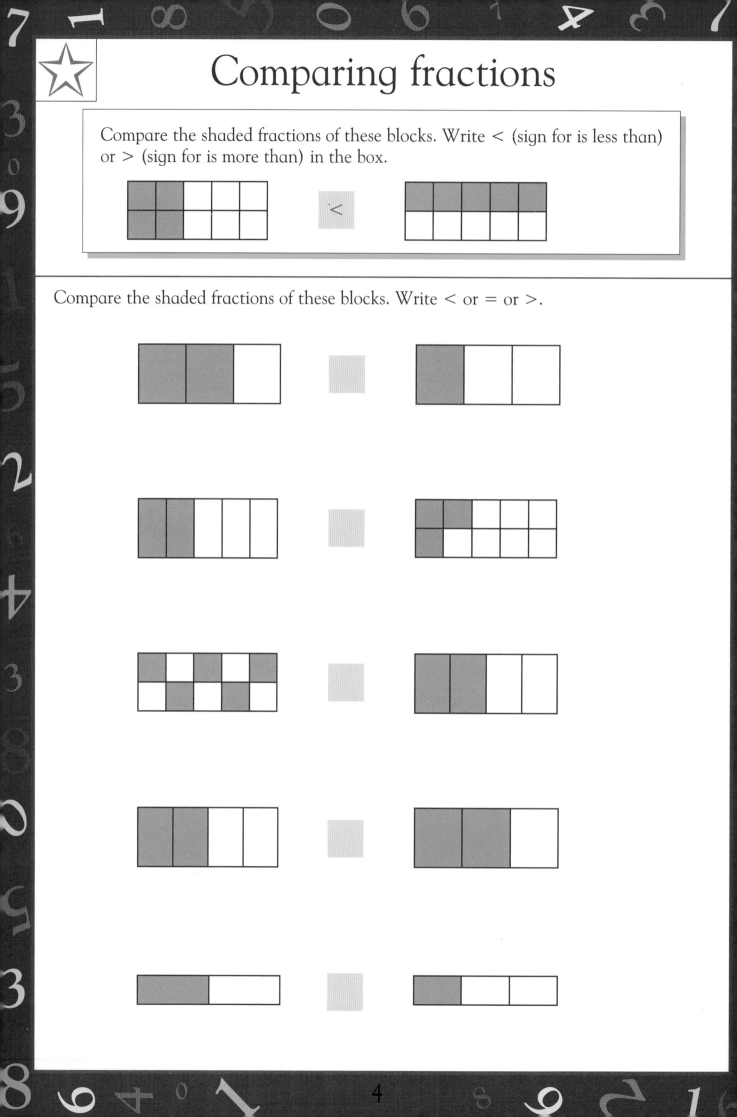

Compare the shaded fractions of these blocks. Write < or = or >.

Simple fractions

What is $\frac{2}{3}$ of 9?

$\frac{1}{3}$ of 9 is 3

So $\frac{2}{3}$ of 9 is 6

What is $\frac{3}{4}$ of 12?

$\frac{1}{4}$ of 12 is 3

So $\frac{3}{4}$ of 12 is 9

What is $\frac{3}{10}$ of 40?

$\frac{1}{10}$ of 40 is 4

So $\frac{3}{10}$ of 40 is 12

What is $\frac{2}{3}$ of each number? Write the answer in the box.

6		15		9		18	
3		12		21		30	
24		33		27		60	

What is $\frac{3}{4}$ of each number? Write the answer in the box.

8		16		4		12	
20		40		28		24	
36		32		44		80	

What is $\frac{3}{10}$ of each number? Write the answer in the box.

60		10		50		90	
20		70		30		80	
100		40		200		500	

What is $\frac{7}{10}$ of each number? Write the answer in the box.

90		50		10		60	
80		30		70		20	
200		500		40		100	

Write the answer in the box.

There are 30 children in a class. Two-thirds of them are boys.
How many of the class are girls?

Out of 70 birds in a zoo, three-tenths are eagles. How many birds are eagles?

Simple fractions

Write the answer in the box.

What fraction of 9 is 3?

$\dfrac{1}{3}$

How much is
one-third of 18p?

6p

How long is a
quarter of an hour?

15 minutes

Write the answer in the box.

What fraction of 8 is 4?

How long is $\dfrac{1}{10}$ of 20 cm?

How much is one-third of £6.00?

What fraction of 20 is 10?

How long is $\dfrac{1}{10}$ of 70 cm?

How much is one-third of 24p?

What fraction of 12 is 3?

How long is half of 30 cm?

How much is one-third of 30p?

What fraction of 10 is 1?

Write the answer in the box.

What fraction of 12 is 4?

How long is $\dfrac{3}{10}$ of 40 cm?

How much is two-thirds of 15p?

What fraction of 18 is 6?

How long is nine-tenths of 60 cm?

How much is two-thirds of 24p?

What fraction of 30 is 3?

How long is one-third of 33 cm?

How much is three-quarters of 40p?

What fraction of 24 is 6?

Write the answer in the box.

What fraction of 100 is 25?

How long is two-thirds of 60 m?

How much is three-quarters of
£1.00?

What fraction of 21 is 7?

How long is $\dfrac{7}{10}$ of 20 km?

How much is three-quarters of 28p?

What fraction of 60 is 40?

How long is two-thirds of 36 m?

How much is three-quarters of 4p?

What fraction of 16 is 12?

Fraction equivalents

Look at the six strips of paper below. They are all the same length, but have been cut into different fractions. You can see that some fractions are the same, although they are written differently.

one whole 1									
$\frac{1}{2}$					$\frac{1}{2}$				
$\frac{1}{3}$			$\frac{1}{3}$			$\frac{1}{3}$			
$\frac{1}{4}$		$\frac{1}{4}$		$\frac{1}{4}$			$\frac{1}{4}$		
$\frac{1}{5}$	$\frac{1}{5}$		$\frac{1}{5}$		$\frac{1}{5}$		$\frac{1}{5}$		
$\frac{1}{10}$	$\frac{1}{10}$	$\frac{1}{10}$	$\frac{1}{10}$	$\frac{1}{10}$	$\frac{1}{10}$	$\frac{1}{10}$	$\frac{1}{10}$	$\frac{1}{10}$	$\frac{1}{10}$

Write the fraction that is the same as a half.

$\frac{1}{2}$ is the same as $\quad \frac{2}{4}$

Look at the strips of paper again. Write the fractions that match.

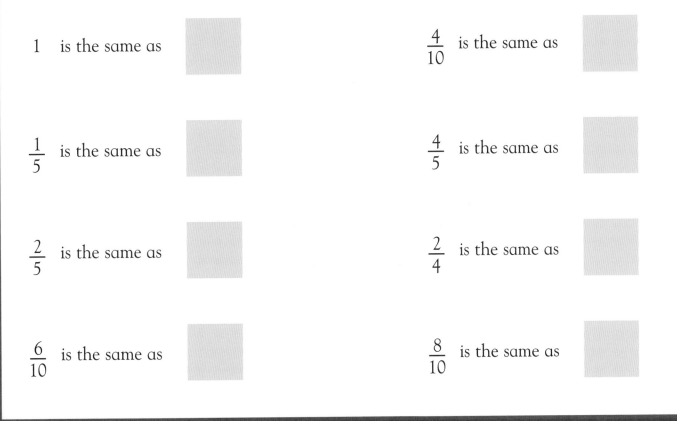

1 is the same as $\frac{4}{10}$ is the same as

$\frac{1}{5}$ is the same as $\frac{4}{5}$ is the same as

$\frac{2}{5}$ is the same as $\frac{2}{4}$ is the same as

$\frac{6}{10}$ is the same as $\frac{8}{10}$ is the same as

Fraction equivalents

Look at the six strips of paper below. They are all the same length, but have been cut into different fractions. You can see that some fractions are the same, although they are written differently.

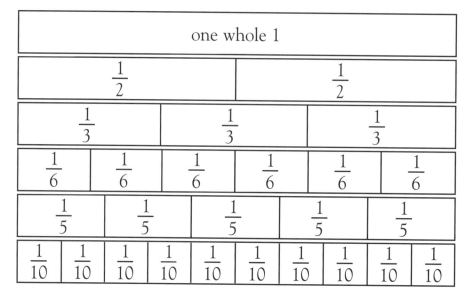

Write the fraction that is the same as a half.

$\frac{1}{2}$ is the same as $\frac{5}{10}$

Look at the strips of paper again. Write the fractions that match.

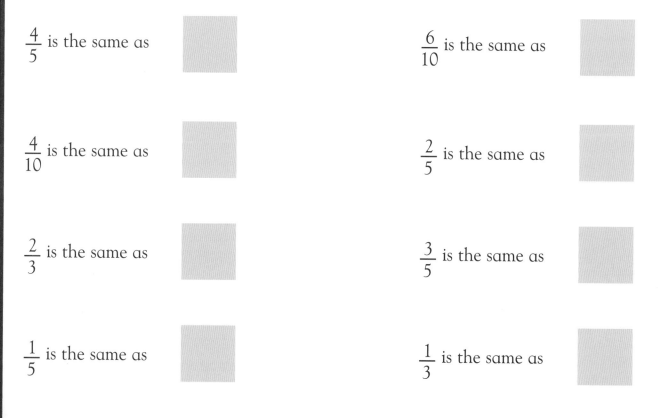

$\frac{4}{5}$ is the same as

$\frac{6}{10}$ is the same as

$\frac{4}{10}$ is the same as

$\frac{2}{5}$ is the same as

$\frac{2}{3}$ is the same as

$\frac{3}{5}$ is the same as

$\frac{1}{5}$ is the same as

$\frac{1}{3}$ is the same as

Adding

Write the answer in the box.

One child has 46 conkers. Another child has 35 conkers.
How many conkers do the children have altogether?

`81`

Write the answer in the box.

Scott has 47p and Moira has
36p. How much do they have
in total?

David has 29p and Katie has
62p. How much do they
have altogether?

Penny skips for 24 seconds and
then Bob skips for 54 seconds.
For how many seconds did they
skip in total?

Dan finds 44p in one pocket and
38p in his other pocket. How
much does he have altogether?

A line is 45 cm long and then
Peta extends it by another 25 cm.
How long is the line now?

What is the sum when 17 is
added to 38?

Three girls add their money
together. They have 26p, 24p,
and 20p. How much do they
have altogether?

A pencil 11 cm long is put end to
end with another pencil 12 cm
long. What is the total length of
the two pencils?

What is the total when 34 is
added to 46?

One child has 47 football cards.
Another has 48 football cards.
How many cards do they have
altogether?

One bag of sweets contains 26
toffees, a second bag contains 19
toffees. How many toffees are
there altogether?

Abel spends 48p on sweets and
then 38p on an ice cream. How
much has Abel spent altogether?

Martha has 45 marbles in one
hand and 56 in the other hand.
How many marbles does Martha
have altogether?

A bag of cherries has 43 ripe
ones and 17 rotten ones. How
many cherries are in the bag?

There are 34 children in one
class and 36 in another. How
many children are there in total?

Adding

Write the answer in the box.

Josh has three piles of bricks. There are 20 bricks in one pile, 18 bricks in the second pile, and 10 bricks in the third pile. How many bricks does Josh have altogether?

48

Write the answer in the box.

What is the total of 13, 17, and 20?

Joanne is given some money at Christmas. She is given £5.00 by Uncle Eddie, £2.50 by Aunt Jo, and £3.50 by her sister. How much is she given in total?

A child receives 32 birthday cards and 77 Christmas cards. How many cards has she received?

How much do these coins add up to: 20p, 50p, 10p, and 5p?

Add together 50p, 20p, and 50p.

What is the sum of 23, 24, and 25?

Jane has three piggy banks. One contains £1.20, the second contains £0.80, and the third contains £3.00. How much does Jane have altogether?

How much is 50p plus 70p plus 80p?

One bag contains 24 grapes, another bag contains 34 grapes, and the third bag contains 30 grapes. What is the total number of grapes?

Bill collects comics. He has 120 but is given 60 more by a friend. How many does Bill have now?

Gill buys three bars of chocolate. One costs 30p, another costs 28p, the third costs 32p. What is the total cost of the chocolate?

What is the total of 60, 70, and 80?

Three containers of sand are delivered to a building site. They weigh 70 kg, 90 kg, and 100 kg. How much do they weigh altogether?

Add together 12 cm, 24 cm, and 36 cm.

A teacher gives out 33 house points on Monday, 25 on Tuesday, and 35 on Wednesday. How many house points have been given out altogether?

Subtracting

Write the answer in the box.

Doris had 40 marbles but then lost 17 in a competition.
How many marbles does Doris have left?

`23`

Write the answer in the box.

I have 35 sweets but then 12 are
eaten. How many sweets are left?

Two numbers add up to 30. One
of the numbers is 18. What is the
other number?

A piece of wood is 60 cm long.
A section 28 cm long is cut off.
How long is the piece
of wood now?

Two numbers add up to 80. One
of the numbers is 45. What is
the other number?

A class has 33 children. 15 of
the class are boys. How many
of the class are girls?

Out of 46 squirrels, 38 are grey
and the rest are red. How many
squirrels are red?

What is 56 less than 100?

A bag contains 60 cherries. 12 of
the cherries are rotten. How
many cherries are not rotten?

Two numbers total 65. One of
the numbers is 32. What is the
other number?

A number added to 15 makes
a total of 40. What number
has been added?

Mary goes shopping with £5.00.
She spends £1.80. How much
does Mary have left?

Dick goes shopping with £5.00.
He returns home with £1.30.
How much has Dick spent?

The sum of two numbers is 80.
One of the numbers is 43.
What is the other number?

A child has 50p pocket money
and gives 24p away to charity.
How much does she have left?

Subtracting

Write the answer in the box.

A road is 35 km long. A section of the road 13 km long has to be repaired. What length of road does not need repair?

22 km

Write the answer in the box.

Shane has to run 100 m. After running 74 metres he trips up. How far did he have left to run?

Samantha has to swim for one hour in a sponsored swim. How much longer must she swim if she has swum for 38 minutes?

Two numbers add up to 80. One of the numbers is 44. What is the other number?

I add 37 to a number and have a total of 66. What is the other number?

A dentist sees 84 patients in a day. If she sees 37 in the morning, how many will she see in the afternoon?

What is the result when I reduce 70 by 33?

A box contains 60 chocolates. 29 are milk the rest are plain. How many chocolates are plain?

A number has been taken away from 90 and the result is 26. What number has been taken away?

What is the total if I reduce 95p by 67p?

A lady grows 100 roses in her garden. 58 of the roses are red and the rest are white. How many of the roses are white?

There are 520 spectators at a football match. 320 are adults and the rest are children. How many are children?

What is the result if I reduce £1.00 by 65p?

Out of 70 sailors, 34 are women. How many are men?

A bag contains 80 marbles. 45 marbles are clear, the rest are coloured. How many are coloured?

A plank of wood is 3.00 m long. It is cut into two sections. One section is 1.20 m long. How long is the other section?

Multiplying

Write the answer in the box.

Amy has six packets of cards. Each packet contains 5 cards. How many cards does Amy have? 30

Write the answer in the box.

Four children have 10p each. How much do they have altogether?

A packet contains 8 pens. John buys 5 packets. How many pens does he have?

What is the result when six is multiplied by four?

Seven children each give 50p to charity. How much have they given altogether?

CHARITY

What number multiplied by 3 makes 120?

How many nines are the same as 45?

A calculator needs three batteries to make it work. How many batteries will be needed to make 10 calculators work?

Five times a number is 30. What is the number?

Rashid multiplies 40p by 5 and believes the answer is £2.00. Is Rashid correct?

Which number multiplied by 4 makes 80?

David believes that eight times four is thirty four. Is he correct?

How many days are there in four weeks?

What is the product of nine and three?

A box contains 8 packets of crisps. How many packets will there be in four boxes?

How much is seven lots of 5p?

Multiplying

Write the answer in the box.

Dan has ten 5p coins. How much money does he have altogether? `50p`

Write the answer in the box.

Which number multiplied by ten gives the answer sixty?

Sarah has four boxes of eggs. Each box contains half a dozen eggs. How many eggs does Sarah have altogether?

A rabbit eats eight carrots a day. How many carrots will five rabbits eat?

Abir thinks that nine fours are 36. Is he correct?

There are six players in a volleyball team. If four teams play each other in a tournament, how many players will there be?

A packet of sweets contains 32 chews. How many sweets are there in three packets?

Children have to write a story four pages long. If twenty children write the story, how many pages will the teacher have to mark?

What is the result when I multiply five by 20?

A case holds 12 bottles of shampoo. How many bottles will there be in 4 cases?

A dog eats 11 cans of food in one week. How many cans of food will the dog eat in five weeks?

Nine times a number is 45. What is the number?

A packet contains 20 tea bags. How many tea bags will there be in five packets?

What number multiplied by seven gives the answer seventy?

June saves 25p each week. How much money does she have at the end of five weeks?

Andy collects twenty 10p coins. How much money does he have altogether?

Dividing

Write the answer in the box. Some will have remainders, some will not.

$34 \div 5 =$ 6 r 4 $20 \div 4 =$ 5

5 r 2
3 $\overline{)\ 17}$

Write the answer in the box. Some will have remainders, some will not.

$37 \div 5 =$ $29 \div 4 =$ $12 \div 5 =$ $33 \div 4 =$

$54 \div 10 =$ $49 \div 5 =$ $3 \div 2 =$ $54 \div 5 =$

$16 \div 4 =$ $38 \div 4 =$ $12 \div 10 =$ $40 \div 4 =$

$31 \div 5 =$ $53 \div 10 =$ $22 \div 3 =$ $17 \div 10 =$

$42 \div 5 =$ $3 \div 3 =$ $20 \div 3 =$ $46 \div 5 =$

Write the answer in the box. Some will have remainders, some will not.

4 $\overline{)\ 17}$ 5 $\overline{)\ 19}$ 3 $\overline{)\ 14}$ 10 $\overline{)\ 44}$

2 $\overline{)\ 23}$ 4 $\overline{)\ 30}$ 5 $\overline{)\ 45}$ 3 $\overline{)\ 29}$

4 $\overline{)\ 23}$ 10 $\overline{)\ 99}$ 2 $\overline{)\ 9}$ 4 $\overline{)\ 25}$

5 $\overline{)\ 36}$ 3 $\overline{)\ 32}$ 10 $\overline{)\ 60}$ 2 $\overline{)\ 5}$

4 $\overline{)\ 80}$ 5 $\overline{)\ 100}$ 3 $\overline{)\ 60}$ 2 $\overline{)\ 100}$

Write the answer in the box.

What is the remainder when 29 is divided by 3?

What is the remainder when 42 is divided by 5?

What is 36 divided by 4?

How many 3s in 33?

What is the result when 40 is divided by 5?

What is the result when 67 is divided by 10?

How many 4s in 36?

How many whole lots of 4 are there in 27?

Dividing

Write the answer in the box.
Dorothy has to share 24 peaches between 3 children.
How many peaches will each child receive?

`8`

Write the answer in the box.

The Wizard shares 32 frogs between 10 monkeys. How many frogs does each monkey receive and how many are left over?

The Tin Man divides 20 cans of oil between 3 clockwork trains. How much goes to each train and how many cans are left over?

The Scarecrow shares out 40 pieces of straw between 5 mice. How many pieces of straw does each mouse receive?

A number divided by 6 is 5. What is the number?

A number multiplied by 4 is 28. What is the number?

How many are left over when 26 is divided by 5?

What is the remainder when 75 is divided by 10?

A father shares a pizza equally between his 3 children. The pizza has 8 sections and the father eats the pieces that are left over. How many pieces does the father eat?

July has 31 days. How many whole weeks are there in July and how many days left over?

A number multiplied by 9 is 36. What is the number?

Two horses share a box of sugar. There are 70 sugar cubes in the box. How many sugar cubes do they each have?

A number divided by 8 is 3. What is the number?

Four children share time on a video game. They have a total time of two minutes. How much time do they each have?

A number divided by 5 gives the result 8. What is the number?

Three mice share 25 lumps of cheese. They give any left-overs to a hamster. How many pieces of cheese does the hamster receive?

What is the remainder when 69 is divided by 7?

Choosing the operation

Write the answer in the box.

I add 25 to a number and the result is 40. What number did I start with? `15`

I reduce a number by 18 and the result is 24. What number did I start with? `42`

Write the answer in the box.

22 is added to a number and the result is 30. What number did I begin with?

I subtract 14 from a number and end up with 17. What number did I start with?

I add 16 to a number and the total of the two numbers is 30. What number did I begin with?

When 26 is subtracted from a number the result is 14. What is the number?

After adding 22 to a number the total is 45. What is the number?

What must you reduce 19 by so that the result is 7?

When 29 is reduced by a certain number, the result is 14. What number has 29 been reduced by?

35 is added to a number and the total is 60. What is the number?

I increase a number by 14 and the total is 30. What number did I start with?

After taking 17 away from a number I am left with 3. What number did I start with?

Paul starts with 50p but spends some money in a shop. He goes home with 18p. How much did Paul spend?

Sue starts out with 23p but is given some money by her auntie. Sue then has 50p. How much was she given?

Alice gives 20p to charity. If she started with 95p, how much does she have left?

Jane has a one-litre bottle of orange and drinks 300 ml. How much does she have left?

A box contains 60 pins and then some are added so that the new total is 85. How many pins have been added?

A tower is made up of 30 bricks. A further 45 are put on the top. How many bricks are in the tower now?

Choosing the operation

Write the answer in the box.

A number is multiplied by 8 and the result is 24. What is the number? `3`

I divide a number by 4 and the answer is 9. What number did I begin with? `36`

Write the answer in the box.

A number is multiplied by 6 and the result is 30. What is the number?

When a number is divided by 7 the result is 4. What is the number?

I multiply a number by 10, and the final number is 70. What number did I multiply?

After dividing a number by 8, I am left with 4. What number did I divide?

When 20 is multiplied by a number the result is 100. What number is used to multiply?

I divide a number by 3 and the result is 9. What is the number?

After multiplying a number by 5, I have 40. What was the number I started with?

When a number is divided by 10 the result is 3. What number was divided?

I multiply a number by 4 and the result is 40. What number was multiplied?

After dividing a number by 2, I am left with 30. What number was divided?

45p is shared equally by some children. Each child receives 9p. How many children are there?

Each box contains 7 felt-tips. I have 28 felt-tips altogether. How many boxes do I have?

I share 80p equally amongst some children. Each child is given 20p. How many children have shared the money?

A bag contains 10 chocolate bars. In all I have 100 chocolate bars. How many bags do I have?

50 peanuts are shared equally between 2 squirrels. How many peanuts does each squirrel receive?

I give £25 to each charity. I give away £200. How many charities did I give money to?

Working with money

Write the total in the box.

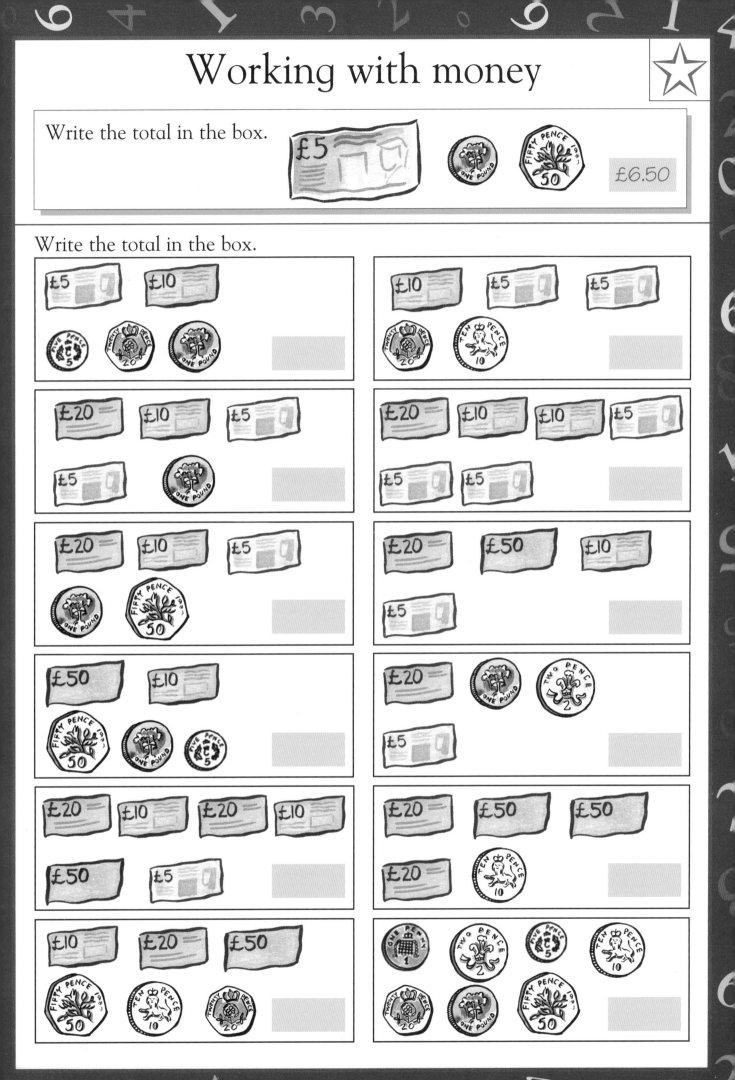

£6.50

Write the total in the box.

Money problems

Write the answer in the box.

Rick goes shopping with a five-pound note. He spends £2.30. How much does Rick have left?

£2.70

Write the answer in the box.

John has three notes. The total value of the notes is £35. Which three notes does he have?

Patrick has a £5 note and a 50p piece. How much more does he need to have £8.00?

After spending £5.50, Ann still has £2.40 left. How much did she start with?

A packet of felt-tips costs £3.45. If Mac pays for them with a £5 note, how much change will he receive?

A man buys a Chinese meal that costs £7.80. He pays for the food with a £10 note. How much change does he receive?

Three pineapples cost a total of £5.10. A lady pays for the pineapples with a £5 note and a £1 coin. How much change does she receive?

Apples cost 60p a kilogram. How much will 4 kilograms cost?

How much change should you receive if you buy food for £8.35 and pay for it with a £10 note?

Jan saves 50p a week for 10 weeks. How much does she have after the ten weeks?

Rob buys a new coat for £34.50 and pays for it with a £50 note. How much change should he receive?

The change given to a lady is £1.50. The lady bought a bag for £8.50. How much did she give to the shopkeeper?

What is the change from £20.00 when a hat is bought for £14.50?

The change from £5.00 is £0.80. How much was spent?

After spending £3.20 on food, a man is given £6.80 change. How much did he give to the shopkeeper?

A box of chocolates costs £6.28. It is paid for with a £5 note and two pound coins. How much extra has been paid?

20

Measuring problems

Write the amount shown on the scale.

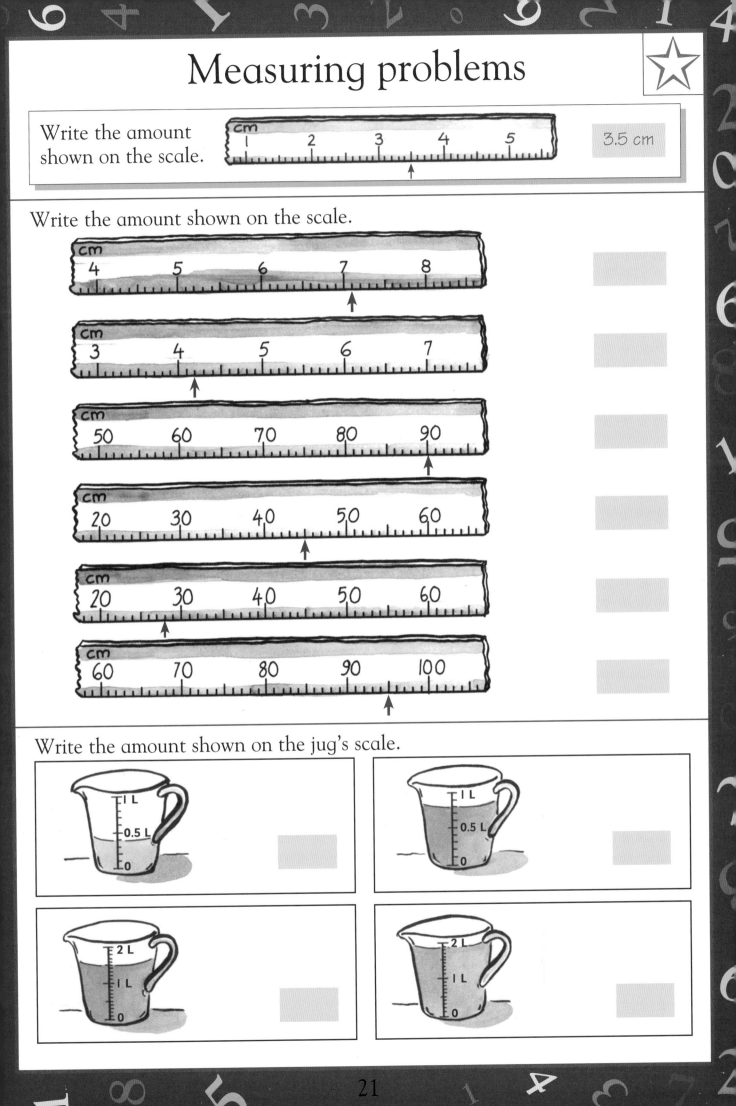

3.5 cm

Write the amount shown on the scale.

Write the amount shown on the jug's scale.

Telling the time

Write the answer in the box. Use words not numbers.

What is the time ten minutes after ten past two?

How long after three o'clock is quarter past three?

What will be the time fifteen minutes after ten to four?

A bus leaves Horndean at 10.05 and arrives
at Winchester 55 minutes later. What
time does the bus arrive in Winchester?

Abir leaves school at 3.35 and takes
20 minutes to walk home. What time does Abir arrive home?

Sandeep puts a cake in the oven at quarter past five. The
cake takes one hour and ten minutes to bake. What time
will Sandeep take the cake out of the oven?

What was the time twenty minutes before quarter past six?

A dog leaves Otterbourne Post Office at twenty past one
and arrives home at ten past two. How long did the dog
take to walk home?

If a man sets out for work at 7.45 and arrives at work at
8.20, how long has his journey taken?

How many minutes after 5.30 is 6.15?

A car ride lasts two and a half hours. If the journey begins
at half past one, what time will it end?

How many minutes before midday is 10.45?

If a trip takes 40 minutes and ends at 11.00, what time
did the trip begin?

Bar charts and pictograms

Look at the bar chart and answer the question.

Number of pets

Which child has three pets? | Paul

Sarah Paul

Look at the bar chart and answer the questions.

Holiday destinations

Number of children

Mexico   Spain   France   Germany England

How many children went to Spain on holiday?

Which country did three children go to?

Which country had fewer children as visitors than Germany?

Which was the most popular country for holidays?

How many children went on holiday?

Look at the pictogram and answer the questions.

Children's favourite hobbies

☺ each face means
2 children

reading sports models games

How many children enjoy models?

Which hobby is enjoyed by 4 children?

How many more children like games than like reading?

Which is the most popular hobby?

More time problems

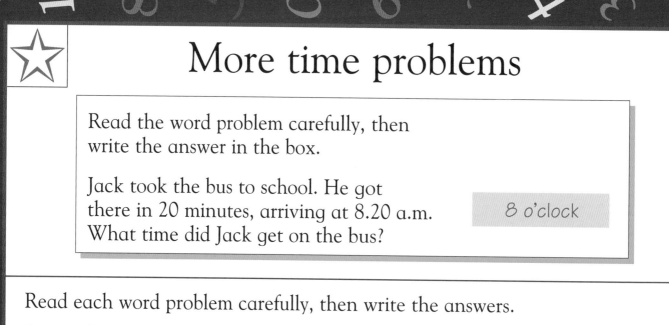

Read the word problem carefully, then write the answer in the box.

Jack took the bus to school. He got there in 20 minutes, arriving at 8.20 a.m. What time did Jack get on the bus?

8 o'clock

Read each word problem carefully, then write the answers.

Gary and Kate are painting the fence.
Gary paints 10 slats in 1 hour. Kate paints 4 slats in 1 hour.

After two hours, how many slats has Gary painted?

How many slats will Kate paint in 2 hours?

How long will it take Gary to paint 30 slats?

Cara can swim across the lake in 40 minutes. Danny can swim across the lake in half that time. How long will it take Danny to swim across the lake?

Jill and her family were hiking up a mountain. They had to hike 4 miles. Jill fell and hurt her knee when they were halfway up. Her family had to take a break and rest.

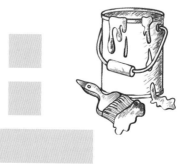

Jill said, "So far, we've hiked [ ] miles up the mountain."

John walks 2 miles to the train in 40 minutes.
Fran walks 3 miles to the train in 45 minutes.

How long does it take John to walk 1 mile?

How long does it take Fran to walk 1 mile?

Who walks faster?

Timetables

Read Mr. Gordon's timetable for Year 4 on Monday below.
Answer the question.

9.00–10.00	10.00–11.30	11.30–12.30	12.35–1.35	1.35–2.30	2.30
English	Maths	Science	Lunch	Social Studies	Dismissal

What time do classes start for Year 4?   *9 o'clock*

Look at Mr. Gordon's timetable again and answer the questions.

When does maths begin?

How long is the science class?

How long is Mr. Gordon's social studies class?

Sunrise Sports Spectacular: Timetable for Saturday's activities

8.30–10.00	10.00–11.30	11.30–12.30	12.35–1.35	1.35–2.30	3.00– 4.15
Swimming	Climbing	Football	Lunch	Tennis	Prizes

Read the timetable for the Sunrise Sports Spectacular. Then answer
the questions that follow.

What is the first activity of the day?

What time is lunch?

What time is tennis played?

How long does football last?

2D shapes

Name each of the shapes.

square   circle

Name each of the shapes.

Draw each shape as carefully as you can.

pentagon

regular hexagon

Sorting 2D shapes

Which shapes have right angles?

1 and 3

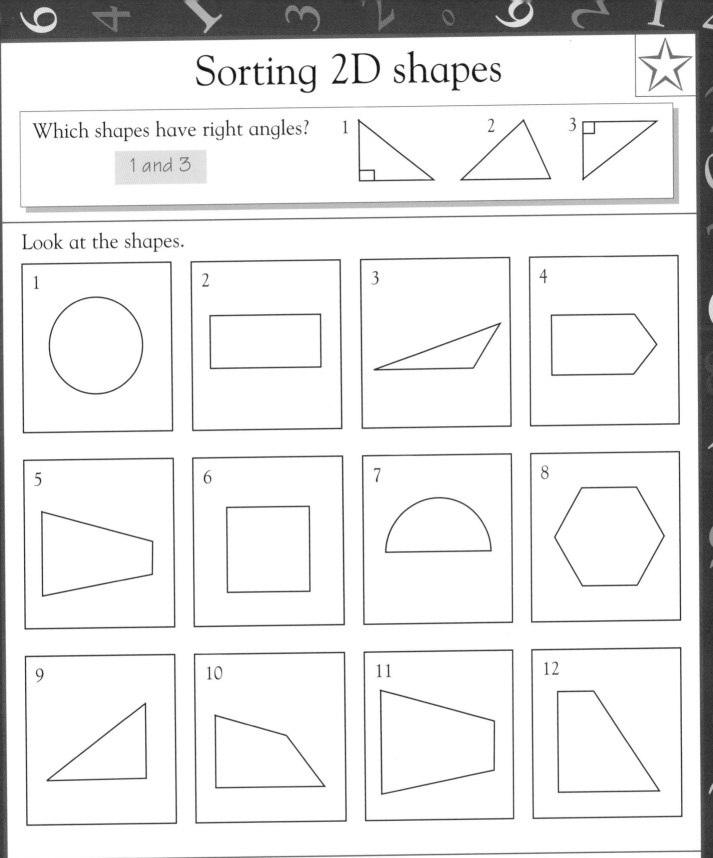

Look at the shapes.

Write the numbers of the shapes in the correct part of the table below.

Shapes with right angles	Shapes without right angles

Symmetry

Does the mirror line show the line of symmetry? Write yes or no.

yes   no   yes

Does the mirror line show the line of symmetry? Write yes or no.

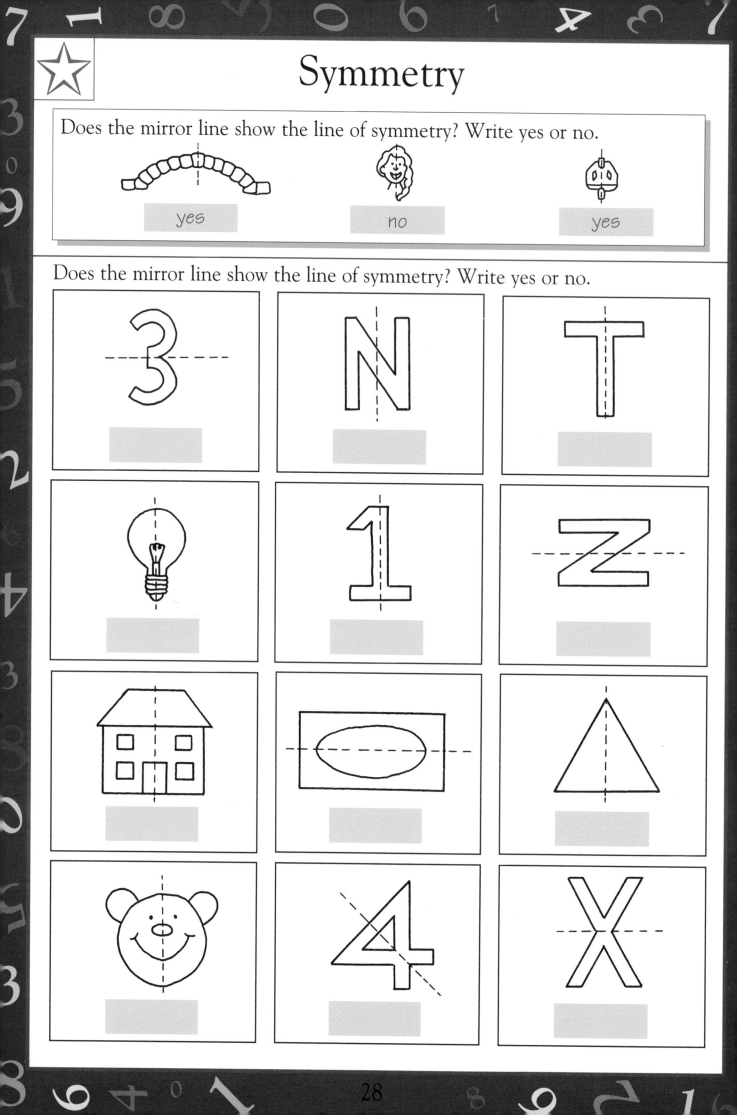

Symmetry

Complete each drawing. The dotted line is the line of symmetry.

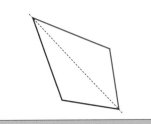 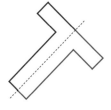 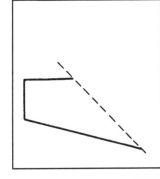

Complete each drawing. The dotted line is the line of symmetry.

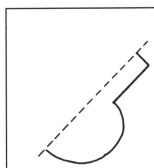 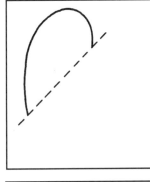 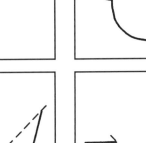 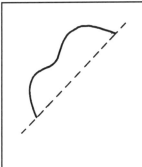

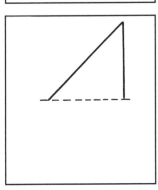 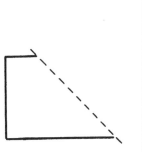 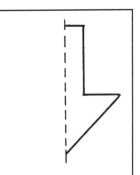 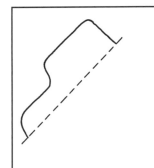

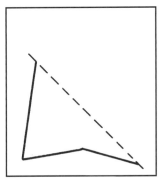 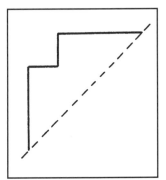 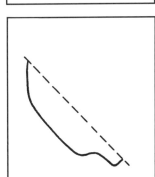 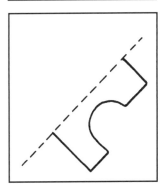

Right angles

Are these angles more or less than a right angle? Write more, less, or right angle.

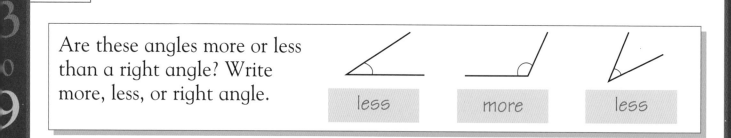

less   more   less

Are these angles more or less than a right angle?
Write more, less, or right angle in the box.

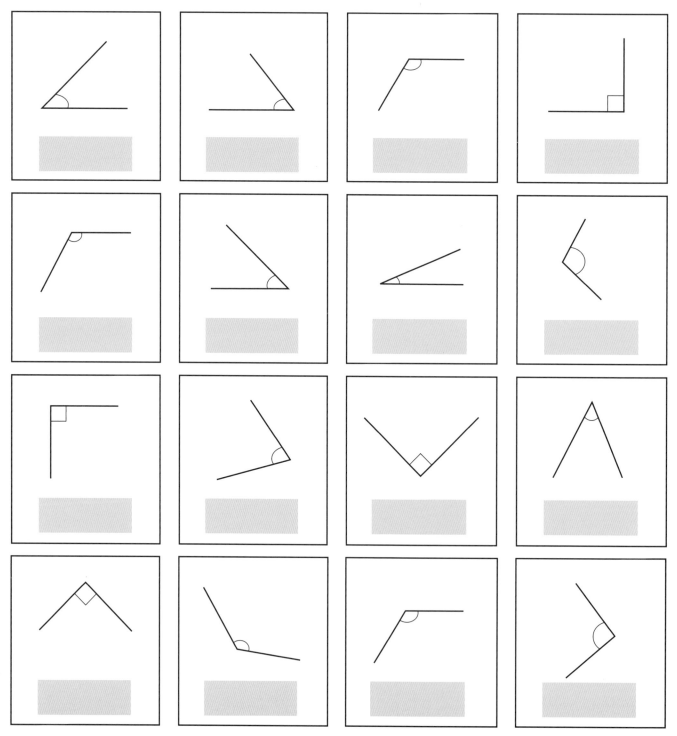

3D shapes

Write the name of each shape in the box.

cuboid   cone   sphere

Write the name of each shape in the box.

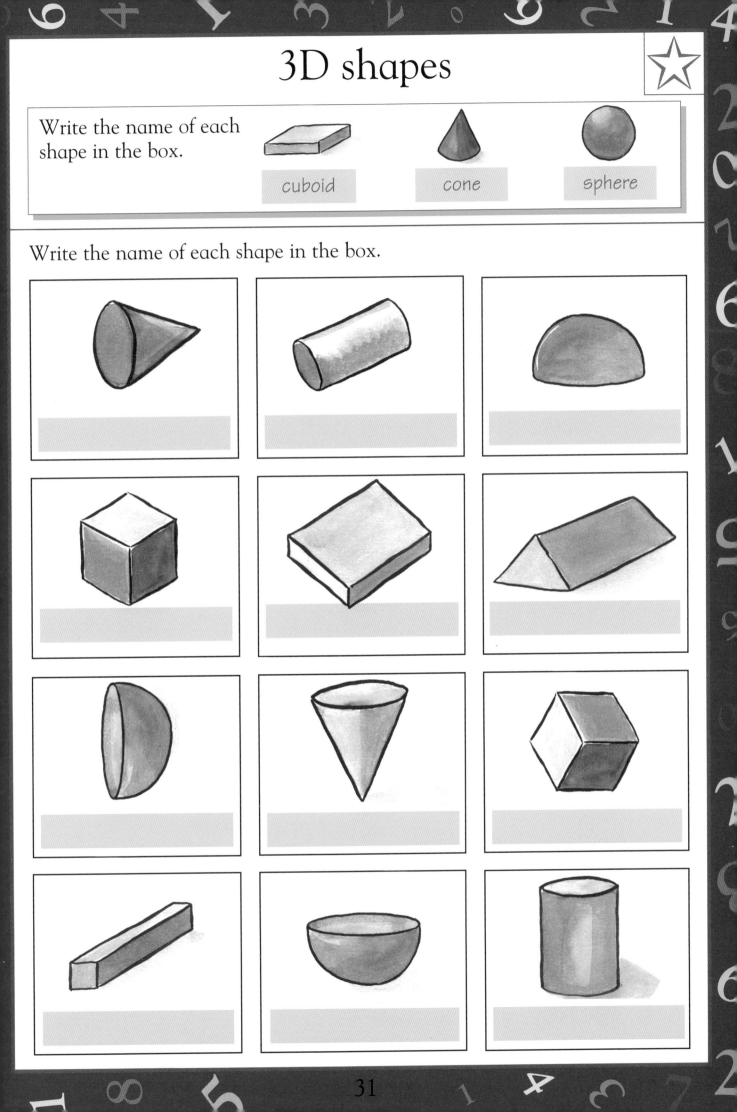

Sorting 3D shapes

Does the shape have a curved surface?

yes

no

Look at these shapes.

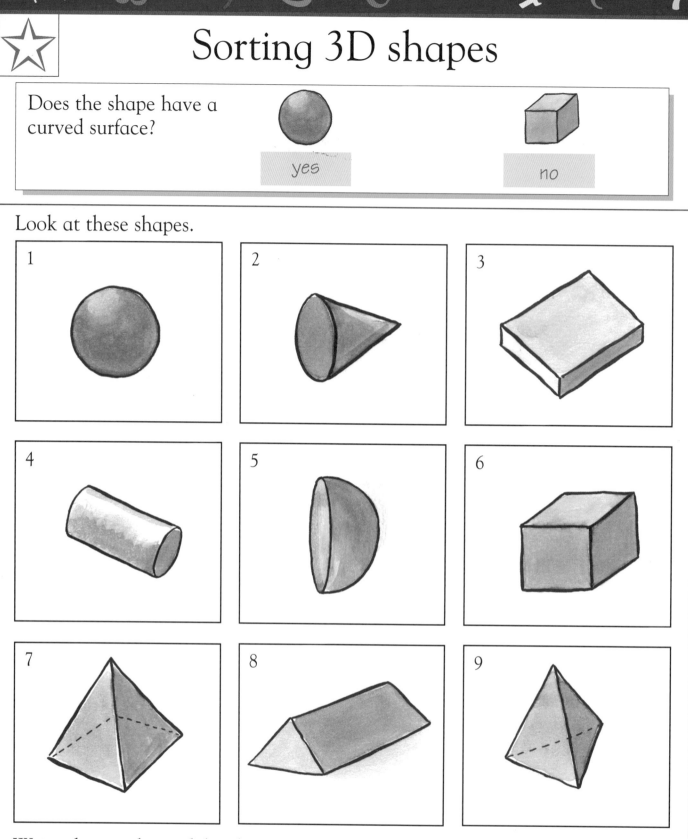

1

2

3

4

5

6

7

8

9

Write the numbers of the shapes in the correct box.

Shapes with curved surfaces	Shapes with no curved surfaces

Answer Section with Parents' Notes

Key Stage 2
Ages 7–8
Advanced

This 8-page section provides answers to all the activities in this book. This will enable you to mark your children's work or it can be used by them if they prefer to do their own marking.

The notes for each page help explain the common pitfalls and problems and, where appropriate, give indications as to what practice is needed to ensure your children understand where they have gone wrong.

Ordering

Write these numbers in order starting with the smallest.

670	760	607	706
607	670	706	760

Write these numbers in order starting with the smallest.

270	720	207	702
207	270	702	720

870	780	807	708
708	780	807	870

906	690	960	609
609	690	906	960

106	610	601	160
106	160	601	610

560	506	650	605
506	560	605	650

849	489	948	984
489	849	948	984

890	980	809	908
809	890	908	980

486	684	864	648
486	648	684	864

405	450	540	504
405	450	504	540

746	647	764	674
647	674	746	764

570	586	490	92
92	490	570	586

76	104	200	92
76	92	104	200

440	66	781	177
66	177	440	781

632	236	77	407
77	236	407	632

842	587	99	88
88	99	587	842

74	101	12	800
12	74	101	800

500	468	395	288
288	395	468	500

600	304	403	89
89	304	403	600

78	9	302	470
9	78	302	470

345	543	53	34
34	53	345	543

The questions that contain zero in the units or tens position may worry children who are uncertain of place value. Children sometimes fail to recognise the two-digit numbers among three-digit numbers and assign to them values they do not have.

Tenths

Write the fractions for the shaded squares on the bar.

$\frac{1}{10}$

$\frac{2}{10}$

Write the fractions for the shaded squares.

$\frac{3}{10}$

$\frac{5}{10}$

$\frac{6}{10}$

$\frac{4}{10}$

$\frac{8}{10}$

Ensure children understand that when you divide something into tenths, you are dividing it into ten equal parts and that each part or fraction is one tenth, which you can write as $\frac{1}{10}$. So two parts can be written as $\frac{2}{10}$, three parts as $\frac{3}{10}$ and so on.

Comparing fractions

Compare the shaded fractions of these blocks. Write < (sign for is less than) or > (sign for is more than) in the box.

<

Compare the shaded fractions of these blocks. Write < or = or >.

>

>

=

<

>

Representing fractions visually by dividing an area up into equal-sized squares, some of which are shaded, makes it much easier for children to compare those fractions. Provide extra practice by making similar patterns of your own on strips of paper.

Simple fractions ⭐

What is $\frac{2}{3}$ of 9?
$\frac{1}{3}$ of 9 is 3
So $\frac{2}{3}$ of 9 is **6**

What is $\frac{3}{4}$ of 12?
$\frac{1}{4}$ of 12 is 3
So $\frac{3}{4}$ of 12 is **9**

What is $\frac{3}{10}$ of 40?
$\frac{1}{10}$ of 40 is 4
So $\frac{3}{10}$ of 40 is **12**

What is $\frac{2}{3}$ of each number? Write the answer in the box.

6	4	15	10	9	6	18	12
3	2	12	8	21	14	30	20
24	16	33	22	27	18	60	40

What is $\frac{3}{4}$ of each number? Write the answer in the box.

8	6	16	12	4	3	12	9
20	15	40	30	28	21	24	18
36	27	32	24	44	33	80	60

What is $\frac{3}{10}$ of each number? Write the answer in the box.

60	18	10	3	50	15	90	27
20	6	70	21	30	9	80	24
100	30	40	12	200	60	500	150

What is $\frac{7}{10}$ of each number? Write the answer in the box.

90	63	50	35	10	7	60	42
80	56	30	21	70	49	20	14
200	140	500	350	40	28	100	70

Write the answer in the box.
There are 30 children in a class. Two-thirds of them are boys.
How many of the class are girls? **10 girls**

Out of 70 birds in a zoo, three-tenths are eagles. How many birds are eagles? **21 eagles**

The questions test whether children understand the method of working out more than '1' part of an amount. The simplest way is to find one part and multiply that result by the required number of parts, e.g. for $\frac{3}{10}$ of 20, find $\frac{1}{10}$ of 20 and multiply that by 3.

⭐ Simple fractions

Write the answer in the box.

What fraction of 9 is 3? **$\frac{1}{3}$**

How much is one-third of 18p? **6p**

How long is a quarter of an hour? **15 minutes**

Write the answer in the box.

What fraction of 8 is 4? **$\frac{1}{2}$** — How much is one-third of 24p? **8p**
How long is $\frac{1}{10}$ of 20 cm? **2 cm** — What fraction of 12 is 3? **$\frac{1}{4}$**
How much is one-third of £6.00? **£2.00** — How long is half of 30 cm? **15 cm**
What fraction of 20 is 10? **$\frac{1}{2}$** — How much is one-third of 30p? **10p**
How long is $\frac{1}{10}$ of 70 cm? **7 cm** — What fraction of 10 is 1? **$\frac{1}{10}$**

Write the answer in the box.

What fraction of 12 is 4? **$\frac{1}{3}$** — How much is two-thirds of 24p? **16p**
How long is $\frac{3}{10}$ of 40 cm? **12 cm** — What fraction of 30 is 3? **$\frac{1}{10}$**
How much is two-thirds of 15p? **10p** — How long is one-third of 33 cm? **11 cm**
What fraction of 18 is 6? **$\frac{1}{3}$** — How much is three-quarters of 40p? **30p**
How long is nine-tenths of 60 cm? **54 cm** — What fraction of 24 is 6? **$\frac{1}{4}$**

Write the answer in the box.

What fraction of 100 is 25? **$\frac{1}{4}$** — How much is three-quarters of 28p? **21p**
How long is two-thirds of 60 m? **40 m** — What fraction of 60 is 40? **$\frac{2}{3}$**
How much is three-quarters of £1.00? **75p** — How long is two-thirds of 36 m? **24 cm**
What fraction of 21 is 7? **$\frac{1}{3}$** — How much is three-quarters of 4p? **3p**
How long is $\frac{7}{10}$ of 20 km? **14 km** — What fraction of 16 is 12? **$\frac{3}{4}$**

This page tests children's understanding of fractions. Questions are worded differently and with different amounts. Questions in the third section are more difficult as they do not revolve around working a basic 'sum'.

Fraction equivalents ⭐

Look at the six strips of paper below. They are all the same length, but have been cut into different fractions. You can see that some fractions are the same, although they are written differently.

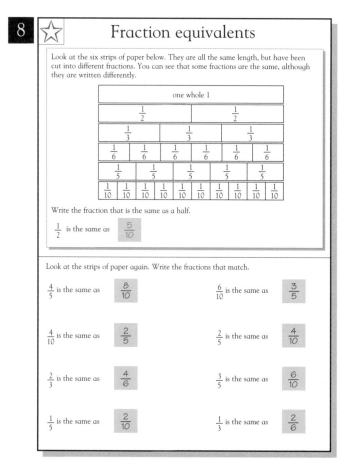

Write the fraction that is the same as a half.

$\frac{1}{2}$ is the same as **$\frac{2}{4}$**

Look at the strips of paper again. Write the fractions that match.

1 is the same as **$\frac{4}{4}$** — $\frac{4}{10}$ is the same as **$\frac{2}{5}$**

$\frac{1}{5}$ is the same as **$\frac{2}{10}$** — $\frac{4}{5}$ is the same as **$\frac{8}{10}$**

$\frac{2}{5}$ is the same as **$\frac{4}{10}$** — $\frac{2}{4}$ is the same as **$\frac{1}{2}$**

$\frac{6}{10}$ is the same as **$\frac{3}{5}$** — $\frac{8}{10}$ is the same as **$\frac{4}{5}$**

This approach allows children to see clearly how the same portion or fraction of something can be written in different ways. Point out that multiplying or dividing both the top and bottom numbers of any fraction by the same number will give an equivalent fraction.

⭐ Fraction equivalents

Look at the six strips of paper below. They are all the same length, but have been cut into different fractions. You can see that some fractions are the same, although they are written differently.

Write the fraction that is the same as a half.

$\frac{1}{2}$ is the same as **$\frac{5}{10}$**

Look at the strips of paper again. Write the fractions that match.

$\frac{4}{5}$ is the same as **$\frac{8}{10}$** — $\frac{6}{10}$ is the same as **$\frac{3}{5}$**

$\frac{4}{10}$ is the same as **$\frac{2}{5}$** — $\frac{2}{5}$ is the same as **$\frac{4}{10}$**

$\frac{2}{3}$ is the same as **$\frac{4}{6}$** — $\frac{3}{5}$ is the same as **$\frac{6}{10}$**

$\frac{1}{5}$ is the same as **$\frac{2}{10}$** — $\frac{1}{3}$ is the same as **$\frac{2}{6}$**

This page involves more practice of the work done on the previous page.

Adding

Write the answer in the box.
One child has 46 conkers. Another child has 35 conkers.
How many conkers do the children have altogether? `81`

Write the answer in the box.

Scott has 47p and Moira has 36p. How much do they have in total? `83p`

David has 29p and Katie has 62p. How much do they have altogether? `91p`

Penny skips for 24 seconds and then Bob skips for 54 seconds. For how many seconds did they skip in total? `78 s`

Dan finds 44p in one pocket and 38p in his other pocket. How much does he have altogether? `82p`

A line is 45 cm long and then Peta extends it by another 25 cm. How long is the line now? `70 cm`

What is the sum when 17 is added to 38? `55`

Three girls add their money together. They have 26p, 24p, and 20p. How much do they have altogether? `70p`

A pencil 11 cm long is put end to end with another pencil 12 cm long. What is the total length of the two pencils? `23 cm`

What is the total when 34 is added to 46? `80`

One child has 47 football cards. Another has 48 football cards. How many cards do they have altogether? `95`

One bag of sweets contains 26 toffees, a second bag contains 19 toffees. How many toffees are there altogether? `45`

Abel spends 48p on sweets and then 38p on an ice cream. How much has Abel spent altogether? `86p`

Martha has 45 marbles in one hand and 56 in the other hand. How many marbles does Martha have altogether? `101`

A bag of cherries has 43 ripe ones and 17 rotten ones. How many cherries are in the bag? `60`

There are 34 children in one class and 36 in another. How many children are there in total? `70`

Ideally children should work out these sums in their heads. If necessary they may work them out on paper. They may use their own methods of calculation as long as their method is accurate, fairly quick, and does not involve adding on fingers.

Adding

Write the answer in the box.
Josh has three piles of bricks. There are 20 bricks in one pile, 18 bricks in the second pile, and 10 bricks in the third pile.
How many bricks does Josh have altogether? `48`

Write the answer in the box.

What is the total of 13, 17, and 20? `50`

Joanne is given some money at Christmas. She is given £5.00 by Uncle Eddie, £2.50 by Aunt Jo, and £3.50 by her sister. How much is she given in total? `£11`

A child receives 32 birthday cards and 77 Christmas cards. How many has she received? `109`

How much do these coins add up to: 20p, 50p, 10p, and 5p? `85p`

Add together 50p, 20p, and 50p. `120p`

What is the sum of 23, 24, and 25? `72`

Jane has three piggy banks. One contains £1.20, the second contains £0.80, and the third contains £3.00. How much does Jane have altogether? `£5.00`

How much is 50p plus 70p plus 80p? `200p`

One bag contains 24 grapes, another bag contains 34 grapes, and the third bag contains 30 grapes. What is the total number of the grapes? `88`

Bill collects comics. He has 120 but is given 60 more by a friend. How many does Bill have now? `180`

Gill buys three bars of chocolate. One costs 30p, another costs 28p, the third costs 32p. What is the total cost of the chocolate? `90p`

What is the total of 60, 70, and 80? `210`

Three containers of sand are delivered to a building site. They weigh 70 kg, 90 kg, and 100 kg. How much do they weigh altogether? `260 kg`

Add together 12 cm, 24 cm, and 36 cm. `72 cm`

A teacher gives out 33 house points on Monday, 25 on Tuesday, and 35 on Wednesday. How many house points have been given out altogether? `93`

Encourage children to work out these problems in their heads. Some of the questions give numbers that bond to produce a tens amount that should assist in the mental process. Children should try to spot such amounts.

Subtracting

Write the answer in the box.
Doris had 40 marbles but then lost 17 in a competition.
How many marbles does Doris have left? `23`

Write the answer in the box.

I have 35 sweets but then 12 are eaten. How many sweets are left? `23`

Two numbers add up to 30. One of the numbers is 18. What is the other number? `12`

A piece of wood is 60 cm long. A section 28 cm long is cut off. How long is the piece of wood now? `32 cm`

Two numbers add up to 80. One of the numbers is 45. What is the other number? `35`

A class has 33 children. 15 of the class are boys. How many of the class are girls? `18`

Out of 46 squirrels, 38 are grey and the rest are red. How many squirrels are red? `8`

What is 56 less than 100? `44`

A bag contains 60 cherries. 12 of the cherries are rotten. How many cherries are not rotten? `48`

Two numbers total 65. One of the numbers is 32. What is the other number? `33`

A number added to 15 makes a total of 40. What number has been added? `25`

Mary goes shopping with £5.00. She spends £1.80. How much does Mary have left? `£3.20`

Dick goes shopping with £5.00. He returns home with £1.30. How much has Dick spent? `£3.70`

The sum of two numbers is 80. One of the numbers is 43. What is the other number? `37`

A child has 50p pocket money and gives 24p away to charity. How much does she have left? `26p`

A common method to help children do sums in their heads is to begin with the lower number and 'add on' until the higher number is reached, e.g. for 35–12, add 8 to 12 to make 20, then 10 to 20 to make 30, then 5 to 30 to make 35, and finally add 8+10+5 to get 23.

Subtracting

Write the answer in the box.
A road is 35 km long. A section of the road 13 km long has to be repaired. What length of road does not need repair? `22 km`

Write the answer in the box.

Shane has to run 100 m. After running 74 metres he trips up. How far did he have left to run? `26 m`

Samantha has to swim for one hour in a sponsored swim. How much longer must she swim if she has swum for 38 minutes? `22 min`

Two numbers add up to 80. One of the numbers is 44. What is the other number? `36`

I add 37 to a number and have a total of 66. What is the other number? `29`

A dentist sees 84 patients in a day. If she sees 37 in the morning, how many will she see in the afternoon? `47`

What is the result when I reduce 70 by 33? `37`

A box contains 60 chocolates. 29 are milk the rest are plain. How many chocolates are plain? `31`

A number has been taken away from 90 and the result is 26. What number has been taken away? `64`

What is the total if I reduce 95p by 67p? `28p`

A lady grows 100 roses in her garden. 58 of the roses are red and the rest are white. How many of the roses are white? `42`

There are 520 spectators at a football match. 320 are adults and the rest are children. How many are children? `200`

What is the result if I reduce £1.00 by 65p? `35p`

Out of 70 sailors, 34 are women. How many are men? `36`

A bag contains 80 marbles. 45 marbles are clear, the rest are coloured. How many are coloured? `35`

A plank of wood is 3.00 m long. It is cut into two sections. One section is 1.20 m long. How long is the other section? `1.80 m`

These questions use different ways of saying 'subtract'. Most of the sums children can work out in their heads using a method similar to that described on the previous page. If necessary, children may work out the sums on paper.

Multiplying

Write the answer in the box.
Amy has six packets of cards. Each packet contains 5 cards.
How many cards does Amy have? `30`

Write the answer in the box.

Four children have 10p each. How much do they have altogether? `40p`

A packet contains 8 pens. John buys 5 packets. How many pens does he have? `40`

What is the result when six is multiplied by four? `24`

Seven children each give 50p to charity. How much have they given altogether? `£3.50`

How many days are there in four weeks? `28`

What is the product of nine and three? `27`

A box contains 8 packets of crisps. How many packets will there be in four boxes? `32`

What number multiplied by 3 makes 120? `40`

How many nines are the same as 45? `5`

A calculator needs three batteries to make it work. How many batteries will be needed to make 10 calculators work? `30`

Five times a number is 30. What is the number? `6`

Rashid multiplies 40p by 5 and believes the answer is £2.00. Is Rashid correct? `yes`

Which number multiplied by 4 makes 80? `20`

David believes that eight times four is thirty four. Is he correct? `no`

How much is seven lots of 5p? `35p`

These questions test children's knowledge of times tables. Watch out for speed of recall as well as accuracy. Children who go through the tables saying 'five, ten, fifteen, etc.' have not yet learned them well enough and need to know the answers by heart.

Multiplying

Write the answer in the box.
Dan has ten 5p coins. How much money does he have altogether? `50p`

Write the answer in the box.

Which number multiplied by ten gives the answer sixty? `6`

Sarah has four boxes of eggs. Each box contains half a dozen eggs. How many eggs does Sarah have altogether? `24`

A rabbit eats eight carrots a day. How many carrots will five rabbits eat? `40`

Abir thinks that nine fours are 36. Is he correct? `yes`

There are six players in a volleyball team. If four teams play each other in a tournament, how many players will there be? `24`

A packet of sweets contains 32 chews. How many sweets are there in three packets? `96`

Children have to write a story four pages long. If twenty children write the story, how many pages will the teacher have to mark? `80`

What is the result when I multiply five by 20? `100`

A case holds 12 bottles of shampoo. How many bottles will there be in 4 cases? `48`

A dog eats 11 cans of food in one week. How many cans of food will the dog eat in five weeks? `55`

Nine times a number is 45. What is the number? `5`

A packet contains 20 tea bags. How many tea bags will there be in five packets? `100`

What number multiplied by seven gives the answer seventy? `10`

June saves 25p each week. How much money does she have at the end of five weeks? `£1.25`

Andy collects twenty 10p coins. How much money does he have altogether? `£2.00`

Though the multiplications on this page may be a little more difficult than on the previous page, children should still be encouraged to work them out in their heads. The twelfth question (20x5) tests whether they know to multiply 5x2 and then add the zero.

Dividing

Write the answer in the box. Some will have remainders, some will not.

$34 \div 5 =$ `6 r 4` $20 \div 4 =$ `5` $3\overline{)17}$ `5 r 2`

Write the answer in the box. Some will have remainders, some will not.

$37 \div 5 =$ `7 r 2` $29 \div 4 =$ `7 r 1` $12 \div 5 =$ `2 r 2` $33 \div 4 =$ `8 r 1`

$54 \div 10 =$ `5 r 4` $49 \div 5 =$ `9 r 4` $3 \div 2 =$ `1 r 1` $54 \div 5 =$ `10 r 4`

$16 \div 4 =$ `4` $38 \div 4 =$ `9 r 2` $12 \div 10 =$ `1 r 2` $40 \div 4 =$ `10`

$31 \div 5 =$ `6 r 1` $53 \div 10 =$ `5 r 3` $22 \div 3 =$ `7 r 1` $17 \div 10 =$ `1 r 7`

$42 \div 5 =$ `8 r 2` $3 \div 3 =$ `1` $20 \div 3 =$ `6 r 2` $46 \div 5 =$ `9 r 1`

Write the answer in the box. Some will have remainders, some will not.

$4\overline{)17}$ `4 r 1` $5\overline{)19}$ `3 r 4` $3\overline{)14}$ `4 r 2` $10\overline{)44}$ `4 r 4`

$2\overline{)23}$ `11 r 1` $4\overline{)30}$ `7 r 2` $5\overline{)45}$ `9` $9\overline{)29}$ `9 r 2`

$4\overline{)23}$ `5 r 3` $10\overline{)99}$ `9 r 9` $2\overline{)9}$ `4 r 1` $4\overline{)25}$ `6 r 1`

$5\overline{)36}$ `7 r 1` $3\overline{)32}$ `10 r 2` $10\overline{)60}$ `6` $2\overline{)5}$ `2 r 1`

$4\overline{)80}$ `20` $5\overline{)100}$ `20` $3\overline{)60}$ `20` $2\overline{)100}$ `50`

Write the answer in the box.

What is the remainder when 29 is divided by 3? `2`

What is 36 divided by 4? `9`

What is the result when 40 is divided by 5? `8`

How many 4s in 36? `9`

What is the remainder when 42 is divided by 5? `2`

How many 3s in 33? `11`

What is the result when 67 is divided by 10? `6 r 7`

How many whole lots of 4 are there in 27? `6`

These division sums test children's times tables knowledge and mental subtraction abilities. Do not encourage the use of pencil and paper except in cases of difficulty. Children should read the third section carefully as some questions are worded differently.

Dividing

Write the answer in the box.
Dorothy has to share 24 peaches between 3 children. How many peaches will each child receive? `8`

Write the answer in the box.

The Wizard shares 32 frogs between 10 monkeys. How many frogs does each monkey receive and how many are left over? `3 r 2`

The Tin Man divides 20 cans of oil between 3 clockwork trains. How much goes to each train and how many cans are left over? `6 r 2`

The Scarecrow shares out 40 pieces of straw between 5 mice. How many pieces of straw does each mouse receive? `8`

A number divided by 6 is 5. What is the number? `30`

A number multiplied by 4 is 28. What is the number? `7`

How many are left over when 26 is divided by 5? `1`

What is the remainder when 75 is divided by 10? `5`

A father shares a pizza equally between his 3 children. The pizza has 8 sections and the father eats the pieces that are left over. How many pieces does the father eat? `2`

July has 31 days. How many whole weeks are there in July and how many days left over? `4 r 3`

A number multiplied by 9 is 36. What is the number? `4`

Two horses share a box of sugar. There are 70 sugar cubes in the box. How many sugar cubes do they each have? `35`

A number divided by 8 is 3. What is the number? `24`

Four children share time on a video game. They have a total time of two minutes. How much time do they each have? `30 s`

A number divided by 5 gives the result 8. What is the number? `40`

Three mice share 25 lumps of cheese. They give any left-overs to a hamster. How many pieces of cheese does the hamster receive? `1`

What is the remainder when 69 is divided by 7? `6`

Children sometimes find questions hard to work out when they are put in word context. Division problems are presented in different ways on this page and are a real test of whether children understand division with and without remainders.

Choosing the operation ⭐

Write the answer in the box.

I add 25 to a number and the result is 40. What number did I start with? **15**

I reduce a number by 18 and the result is 24. What number did I start with? **42**

Write the answer in the box.

22 is added to a number and the result is 30. What number did I begin with? **8**

I subtract 14 from a number and end up with 17. What number did I start with? **31**

I add 16 to a number and the total of the two numbers is 30. What number did I begin with? **14**

When 26 is subtracted from a number the result is 14. What is the number? **40**

After adding 22 to a number the total is 45. What is the number? **23**

What must you reduce 19 by so that the result is 7? **12**

When 29 is reduced by a certain number, the result is 14. What number has 29 been reduced by? **15**

35 is added to a number and the total is 60. What is the number? **25**

I increase a number by 14 and the total is 30. What number did I start with? **16**

After taking 17 away from a number I am left with 3. What number did I start with? **20**

Paul starts with 50p but spends some money in a shop. He goes home with 18p. How much did Paul spend? **32p**

Sue starts out with 23p but is given some money by her auntie. Sue then has 50p. How much was she given? **27p**

Alice gives 20p to charity. If she started with 95p, how much has she left? **75p**

Jane has a one-litre bottle of orange and drinks 300 ml. How much does she have left? **700 ml**

A box contains 60 pins and then some are added so that the new total is 85. How many pins have been added? **25**

A tower is made up of 30 bricks. A further 45 are put on the top. How many bricks are in the tower now? **75**

These questions test children's ability to choose the right operation – addition or subtraction. Many children who are able to do sums written in the traditional form are unsure when they are put into word context. Children who get many of these wrong will need more practice.

Choosing the operation

Write the answer in the box.

A number is multiplied by 8 and the result is 24. What is the number? **3**

I divide a number by 4 and the answer is 9. What number did I begin with? **36**

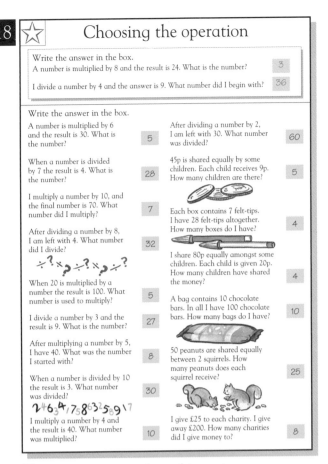

Write the answer in the box.

A number is multiplied by 6 and the result is 30. What is the number? **5**

When a number is divided by 7 the result is 4. What is the number? **28**

I multiply a number by 10, and the final number is 70. What number did I multiply? **7**

After dividing a number by 8, I am left with 4. What number did I divide? **32**

When 20 is multiplied by a number the result is 100. What number is used to multiply? **5**

I divide a number by 3 and the result is 9. What is the number? **27**

After multiplying a number by 5, I have 40. What was the number I started with? **8**

When a number is divided by 10 the result is 3. What number was divided? **30**

I multiply a number by 4 and the result is 40. What number was multiplied? **10**

After dividing a number by 2, I am left with 30. What number was divided? **60**

45p is shared equally by some children. Each child receives 9p. How many children are there? **5**

Each box contains 7 felt-tips. I have 28 felt-tips altogether. How many boxes do I have? **4**

I share 80p equally amongst some children. Each child is given 20p. How many children have shared the money? **4**

A bag contains 10 chocolate bars. In all I have 100 chocolate bars. How many bags do I have? **10**

50 peanuts are shared equally between 2 squirrels. How many peanuts does each squirrel receive? **25**

I give £25 to each charity. I give away £200. How many charities did I give money to? **8**

These questions are phrased in various ways so children need to decide on whether to multiply or divide. They can usually work out sums when the times or divide signs are given but find it more difficult to choose between operations.

Working with money ⭐

Write the total in the box. £5 ... £1 ... 50 **£6.50**

Write the total in the box.

£5 £10 ... £16.25

£10 £5 £5 ... £20.30

£20 £10 £5 / £5 ... £41

£20 £10 £10 £5 / £5 £5 ... £55

£20 £10 £5 / 50 ... £36.50

£20 £50 £10 / £5 £5 ... £85

£50 £10 / 50 ... £61.55

£20 / £5 ... £26.02

£20 £10 £20 £10 / £50 £5 ... £115

£20 £50 £50 / £20 ... £140.10

£10 £20 £50 / 50 ... £80.80

... ... £1.88

Some of the notes used in these questions may be unfamiliar to children. The additions are fairly simple but children should check their answers. An easy way to check is to add the amounts from left to right, and then from right to left, and see if the two totals match.

Money problems

Write the answer in the box.
Rick goes shopping with a five-pound note. He spends £2.30. How much does Rick have left? **£2.70**

Write the answer in the box.

John has three notes. The total value of the notes is £35. Which three notes does he have? **£20, £10, £5**

Patrick has a £5 note and a 50p piece. How much more does he need to have £8.00? **£2.50**

After spending £5.50, Ann still has £2.40 left. How much did she start with? **£7.90**

A packet of felt-tips costs £3.45. If Mac pays for them with a £5 note, how much change will he receive? **£1.55**

A man buys a Chinese meal that costs £7.80. He pays for the food with a £10 note. How much change does he receive? **£2.20**

Three pineapples cost a total of £5.10. A lady pays for the pineapples with a £5 note and a £1 coin. How much change does she receive? **£0.90**

Apples cost 60p a kilogram. How much will 4 kilograms cost? **£2.40**

How much change should you receive if you buy food for £8.35 and pay for it with a £10 note? **£1.65**

Jan saves 50p a week for 10 weeks. How much does she have after the ten weeks? **£5.00**

Rob buys a new coat for £34.50 and pays for it with a £50 note. How much change should he receive? **£15.50**

The change given to a lady is £1.50. The lady bought a bag for £8.50. How much did she give to the shopkeeper? **£10.00**

What is the change from £20.00 when a hat is bought for £14.50? **£5.50**

The change from £5.00 is £0.80. How much was spent? **£4.20**

After spending £3.20 on food, a man is given £6.80 change. How much did he give to the shopkeeper? **£10.00**

A box of chocolates costs £6.28. It is paid for with a £5 note and two pound coins. How much extra has been paid? **72p**

These questions involve money in realistic situations. Children should work these sums out in their heads as far as possible.

Measuring problems

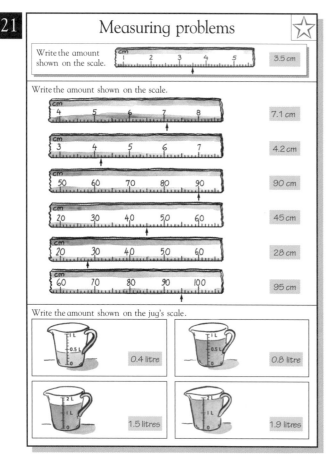

Write the amount shown on the scale.

`cm 1 2 3 4 5` — 3.5 cm

Write the amount shown on the scale.

`cm 4 5 6 7 8` — 7.1 cm

`3 4 5 6 7` — 4.2 cm

`cm 50 60 70 80 90` — 90 cm

`cm 20 30 40 50 60` — 45 cm

`cm 20 30 40 50 60` — 28 cm

`cm 60 70 80 90 100` — 95 cm

Write the amount shown on the jug's scale.

0.4 litre

0.8 litre

1.5 litres

1.9 litres

Children should be able to read off scales of this type relatively easy. Alternative presentation of answers is allowed, e.g. 0.9 m could be .9 m, 0.90 m or 90 cm.

Telling the time

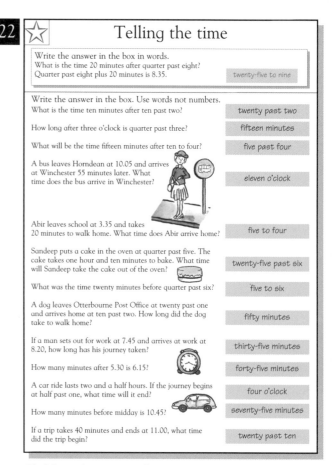

Write the answer in the box in words.
What is the time 20 minutes after quarter past eight?
Quarter past eight plus 20 minutes is 8.35. — twenty-five to nine

Write the answer in the box. Use words not numbers.
What is the time ten minutes after ten past two? — twenty past two

How long after three o'clock is quarter past three? — fifteen minutes

What will be the time fifteen minutes after ten to four? — five past four

A bus leaves Horndean at 10.05 and arrives at Winchester 55 minutes later. What time does the bus arrive in Winchester? — eleven o'clock

Abir leaves school at 3.35 and takes 20 minutes to walk home. What time does Abir arrive home? — five to four

Sandeep puts a cake in the oven at quarter past five. The cake takes one hour and ten minutes to bake. What time will Sandeep take the cake out of the oven? — twenty-five past six

What was the time twenty minutes before quarter past six? — five to six

A dog leaves Otterbourne Post Office at twenty past one and arrives home at ten past two. How long did the dog take to walk home? — fifty minutes

If a man sets out for work at 7.45 and arrives at work at 8.20, how long has his journey taken? — thirty-five minutes

How many minutes after 5.30 is 6.15? — forty-five minutes

A car ride lasts two and a half hours. If the journey begins at half past one, what time will it end? — four o'clock

How many minutes before midday is 10.45? — seventy-five minutes

If a trip takes 40 minutes and ends at 11.00, what time did the trip begin? — twenty past ten

Children do not need to write 'minutes' each time. Subtracting and adding on amounts of time can be difficult for some children when the calculation requires them to cross over the hour boundary.

Bar charts and pictograms

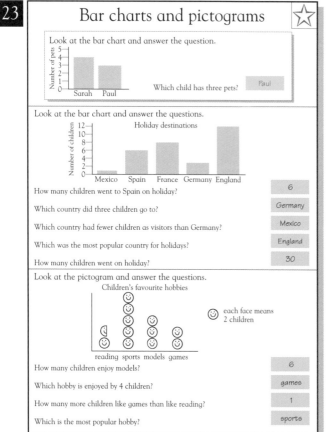

Look at the bar chart and answer the question.

Number of pets — Sarah, Paul

Which child has three pets? — Paul

Look at the bar chart and answer the questions.

Holiday destinations — Number of children — Mexico, Spain, France, Germany, England

How many children went to Spain on holiday? — 6

Which country did three children go to? — Germany

Which country had fewer children as visitors than Germany? — Mexico

Which was the most popular country for holidays? — England

How many children went on holiday? — 30

Look at the pictogram and answer the questions.

Children's favourite hobbies

each face means 2 children

reading sports models games

How many children enjoy models? — 6

Which hobby is enjoyed by 4 children? — games

How many more children like games than like reading? — 1

Which is the most popular hobby? — sports

The bar chart is graded in twos not ones. Children should recognise this and allow for it when working out amounts. The same is the case with the pictogram, where each face represents two children not one.

More time problems

Read the word problem carefully, then write the answer in the box.

Jack took the bus to school. He got there in 20 minutes, arriving at 8.20 a.m. What time did Jack get on the bus? — 8 o'clock

Read each word problem carefully, then write the answers.

Gary and Kate are painting the fence.
Gary paints 10 slats in 1 hour. Kate paints 4 slats in 1 hour.

After two hours, how many slats has Gary painted? — 20

How many slats will Kate paint in 2 hours? — 8

How long will it take Gary to paint 30 slats? — 3 hours

Cara can swim across the lake in 40 minutes. Danny can swim across the lake in half that time. How long will it take Danny to swim across the lake? — 20 minutes

Jill and her family were hiking up a mountain. They had to hike 4 miles. Jill fell and hurt her knee when they were halfway up. Her family had to take a break and rest.

Jill said, "So far, we've hiked 2 miles up the mountain."

John walks 2 miles to the train in 40 minutes.
Fran walks 3 miles to the train in 45 minutes.

How long does it take John to walk 1 mile? — 20 minutes

How long does it take Fran to walk 1 mile? — 15 minutes

Who walks faster? — Fran

When working out time problems, provide children with an analogue clock so they can see the hours and minutes go by. That will help them to connect the word problem with the visual representation of time.

Timetables

Read Mr. Gordon's timetable for Year 4 on Monday below.
Answer the question.

9.00–10.00	10.00–11.30	11.30–12.30	12.35–1.35	1.35–2.30	2.30
English	Maths	Science	Lunch	Social Studies	Dismissal

What time do classes start for Year 4?   9 o'clock

Look at Mr. Gordon's timetable again and answer the questions.

When does maths begin?   10 o'clock

How long is the science class?   1 hour

How long is Mr. Gordon's social studies class?   55 minutes

Sunrise Sports Spectacular: Timetable for Saturday's activities

8.30–10.00	10.00–11.30	11.30–12.30	12.35–1.35	1.35–2.30	3.00– 4.15
Swimming	Climbing	Football	Lunch	Tennis	Prizes

Read the timetable for the Sunrise Sports Spectacular. Then answer the questions that follow.

What is the first activity of the day?   swimming

What time is lunch?   12.35

What time is tennis played?   1.35

How long does football last?   1 hour

Encourage children to try reading different types of timetables. Have them attempt to read train and cinema timetables to get accustomed to the different ways in which such information can be presented.

2D shapes

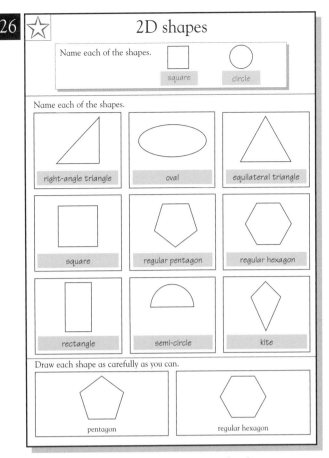

Name each of the shapes.
square   circle

Name each of the shapes.

right-angle triangle   oval   equilateral triangle

square   regular pentagon   regular hexagon

rectangle   semi-circle   kite

Draw each shape as carefully as you can.

pentagon   regular hexagon

Look for accuracy in the answers. The first triangle is a right-angle triangle and the next one is equilateral. The fifth and sixth answers should have 'regular' in front to differentiate them from the irregular variety.

Sorting 2D shapes

Which shapes have right angles?   1   2   3
1 and 3

Look at the shapes.

1   2   3   4

5   6   7   8

9   10   11   12

Write the numbers of the shapes in the correct part of the table below.

Shapes with right angles	Shapes without right angles
2, 4, 6, 9, 10, and 12	1, 3, 5, 7, 8, and 11

Children should be able to recognise right angles in these shapes. If they miss out any just talk it through and give a few more examples.

Symmetry

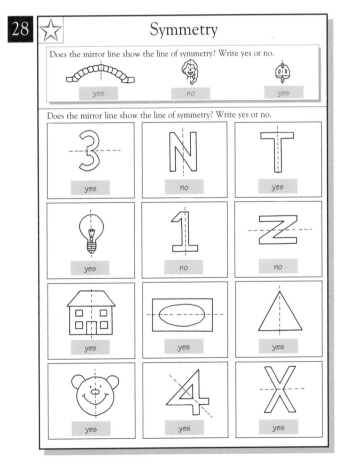

Does the mirror line show the line of symmetry? Write yes or no.
yes   no   yes

Does the mirror line show the line of symmetry? Write yes or no.

yes   no   yes

yes   no   no

yes   yes   yes

yes   yes   yes

Some of these shapes have lines of symmetry in unusual positions. Others are commonly given lines of symmetry when they should not be. Let children use mirrors on the shapes about which they are unsure.

Symmetry

Complete each drawing. The dotted line is the line of symmetry.

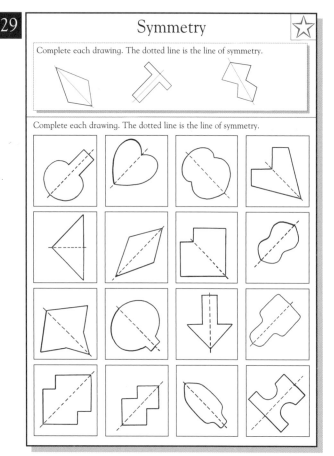

Complete each drawing. The dotted line is the line of symmetry.

Allow children to turn the page so that the line of symmetry is either horizontal or vertical. If they are really unsure let them use a mirror.

Right angles

Are these angles more or less than a right angle? Write more, less, or right angle.

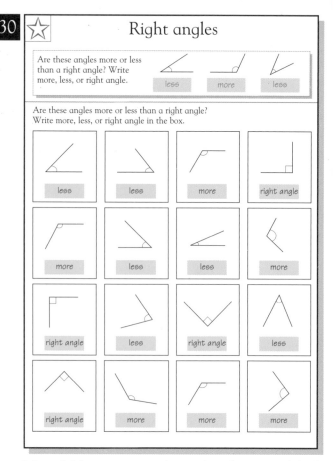

less   more   less

Are these angles more or less than a right angle? Write more, less, or right angle in the box.

less	less	more	right angle
more	less	less	more
right angle	less	right angle	less
right angle	more	more	more

Most children recognise the angles when one of the lines is horizontal. If none of the lines is horizontal, children may be confused. Permit them to move the paper around. You might like to use the words acute (less than 90°) and obtuse (more than 90°, less than 180°).

3D shapes

Write the name of each shape in the box.

cuboid   cone   sphere

Write the name of each shape in the box.

cone	cylinder	hemisphere
cube	cuboid	prism
hemisphere	cone	cube
cuboid	hemisphere	cylinder

Children may be uncertain of prism and hemisphere, especially where the hemisphere is in a different orientation.

Sorting 3D shapes

Does the shape have a curved surface?

yes   no

Look at these shapes.

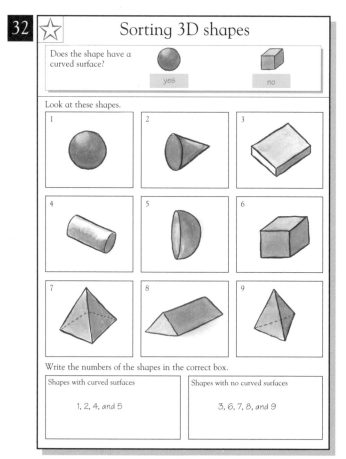

Write the numbers of the shapes in the correct box.

Shapes with curved surfaces	Shapes with no curved surfaces
1, 2, 4, and 5	3, 6, 7, 8, and 9

Children should find this simple sorting method straightforward. If problems are encountered it is best to find some 3D models or household objects to work with.